SCIENCE FAIR PROJECTS

Plants

Patricia Whitehouse

Heinemann Library
Chicago, Illinois

Produced for Heinemann Library by White-Thomson Publishing Ltd.
Page layout by Tim Mayer and Alison Walper
Edited by Brian Fitzgerald
Photo research by Amy Sparks
Illustrations by Cavedweller Studio
Printed and bound in China by Leo Paper Group

12 11 10 09 08
10 9 8 7 6 5 4 3 2 1

Library of Congress Cataloging-in-Publication Data
Whitehouse, Patricia, 1958–
    Plants / Patricia Whitehouse. — 1st ed.
        p. cm. — (Science fair projects)
    Includes bibliographical references and index.
    ISBN 978-1-4034-7918-1 (hc)
    1. Botany projects—Juvenile literature. 2. Botany—Experiments—Juvenile
literature. 3. Plants—Experiments—Juvenile literature. I. Title.
    QK52.6.W48 2007
    580—dc22

2006039547

Acknowledgments
The author and publishers are grateful to the following for permission to reproduce copyright
material: AGStockUSA, Inc./Alamy **p. 24;** Corbis, Masterfile **p. 4** (Andrew Douglas), 36 (George
H. H. Huey); iStockphoto.com, **title page, pp. 20, 12** (Hazel Proudlove), 16 (Arpad Benedek), 28
(Guy Erwood); Photolibrary **pp. 8** (OSF), 32 (Mark Bolton), 40 (Photononstop)

Cover photograph reproduced with permission of istockphoto.com.

The publishers would like to thank Sue Glass for her assistance in the preparation of this book.

Every effort has been made to contact copyright holders of any material reproduced
in this book. Any omissions will be rectified in subsequent printings if notice is given
to the publisher.

Disclaimer
All the Internet addresses (URLs) given in this book were valid at the time of going to press.
However, due to the dynamic nature of the Internet, some addresses may have changed, or
sites may have changed or ceased to exist since publication. While the author and publisher
regret any inconvenience this may cause readers, no responsibility for any such changes can be
accepted by either the author or the publisher.

 Some words are shown in bold, **like this.** You can
find the definitions for these words in the glossary.

Contents

Science Fair Basics

Starting a science fair project can be an exciting challenge. You can test **scientific theory** by developing an appropriate scientific question. Then you can search, using the thoughtful steps of a well-planned experiment, for the answer to that question. It's like a treasure hunt of the mind.

In a way, your mission is to better understand how your world and the things in it work. You may be rewarded with a good grade or an award for your scientific hard work. But no matter what scores your project receives, you'll be a winner. That's because you will know a little bit more about your subject than you did before you started.

In this book, we'll look at nine science fair projects related to plants and how they grow. We'll find out some amazing things about plants, plant parts, and ways to affect how plants grow.

Do Your Research

Is there something about seeds and plants you've always wondered about? Something you don't quite understand but would like to? Then do a little research about the subject. Go to the library and check out books about the subject that interests you.

Use your favorite Internet search engine to find reliable online sources. Museums, universities, scientific journals, newspapers, and magazines are among the best sources for accurate research. Each experiment in this book lists some suggestions for further research.

The Experiments

Project Information

The beginning of each experiment contains a box like this.

Possible Question:

This question is a suggested starting point for your experiment. You will need to adapt the question to reflect your own interests.

Possible Hypothesis:

Don't worry if your hypothesis doesn't match the one listed here; this is only a suggestion.

Approximate Cost of Materials:

Discuss this with your parents before beginning work.

Materials Needed:

Make sure you can easily get all the materials listed and gather them before beginning work.

Level of Difficulty:

There are three levels of experiments in this book: Easy, Intermediate, and Advanced. The level of difficulty is based on how long the experiment takes and how complicated it is.

When doing research you need to make sure your sources are reliable. Ask yourself the following questions about sources, especially those you find online.

1) How old is the source? Is it possible that the information is outdated?

2) Who wrote the source? Is there an identifiable author, and is the author qualified to write about the topic?

3) What is the purpose of the source? The website of a potato chip company is probably not the best place to look for information on healthful diets.

4) Is the information well documented? Can you tell where the author got his or her information?

Some websites allow you to "chat" online with experts. Make sure you discuss this with your parent or teacher before participating. Never give out private information, including your address or phone number, online.

Continued →

Plants are a great subject for science fair projects. Plants are inexpensive and easy to maintain. They react in interesting ways to light, temperature, and gravity.

Once you know a bit more about the subject you want to explore, you'll be ready to ask a science project question and form an intelligent **hypothesis.** A hypothesis is an educated guess about what the results of your experiment will be. Finally, you'll be ready to begin your science fair exploration!

What Is an Experiment?

When you say you're going to "experiment," you may just mean that you're going to try something out. When a scientist uses that word, though, he or she means something else. In a proper experiment, you have **variables** and a **control.** A variable is something that changes. The independent variable is the thing you purposely change as part of the experiment. The dependent variable is the change that happens in response to the thing you do. The controlled variables, or control group, are the things you do not change so that you have something to compare your outcomes with. Here's an example: You want to test whether fertilizer really helps grass grow. You add fertilizer to three plastic cups of grass seed (Group A). You do not add fertilizer to three other cups of grass seed (Group B). Group A is the independent variable. The effect of the fertilizer is the dependent variable. Group B is the control group. Using a large sample of cups for both the variable and control groups will ensure that the results of your experiment are accurate.

Some of the projects in this book are not proper experiments. They are projects designed to help you learn about a subject. You need to check with your teacher about whether these projects are appropriate for your science fair. Before beginning a project, make sure you know the rules about what kinds of projects and materials are allowed.

Your Hypothesis

Once you've decided what question you're going to try to answer, you'll want to make a scientific **prediction** of what you'll discover through your science project. For example, if you notice that plants don't grow much in the winter, your question might be, "Does temperature affect how fast plants grow?"

Remember, your hypothesis states the results you expect from your experiment. So your hypothesis in response to the above question might be, "Plants grow more slowly at lower temperatures." Your research question also offers a good way to find out whether you can actually complete the steps needed for a successful project. If your question is, "How many seeds are there in the world?," it will be impossible to test your hypothesis, no matter how you express it. So, be sure the evidence to support your hypothesis is actually within reach.

Research Journal

It is very important to keep careful notes about your project. From start to finish, make entries in your research journal so you won't have to rely on memory when it is time to create your display. What time did you start your experiment? How long did you work on it each day? What were the variables, or things that changed, about your experimental setting? How did they change and why? What things did you overlook in planning your project? How did you solve the problems, once you discovered them?

These are the kinds of questions you'll answer in your research journal. No detail is too small when it comes to scientific research. On pages 44–46 of this book, you'll find some tips on writing your report and preparing a winning display. Use these and the tips in each project as guides, but don't be afraid to get creative. Make your display, and your project, your own.

Seeds and Gravity

Seeds are the beginning of life for many plants. When the seeds are in the ground, how do they know which way to grow? Do the stems always grow up, and do the roots always grow down? Does it make a difference whether the seeds are planted right side up or upside down? This experiment will help you find out.

Do Your Research

Plants can grow or bend as a reaction to changes in their environment. The responses are called **tropisms.** Before you begin this project, do some research on plants and **geotropism,** a plant's reaction to gravity. Once you've done some research, you can dig into this project. Or, you may come up with your own unique project after you've read and learned more about the topic.

Here are some books and websites you could start with in your research:

» Hopkins, William G. *Plant Development.* New York: Chelsea House, 2006.

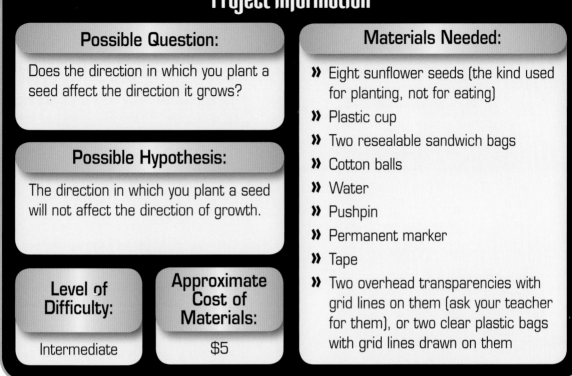

Project Information

Possible Question:

Does the direction in which you plant a seed affect the direction it grows?

Possible Hypothesis:

The direction in which you plant a seed will not affect the direction of growth.

Level of Difficulty:

Intermediate

Approximate Cost of Materials:

$5

Materials Needed:

» Eight sunflower seeds (the kind used for planting, not for eating)
» Plastic cup
» Two resealable sandwich bags
» Cotton balls
» Water
» Pushpin
» Permanent marker
» Tape
» Two overhead transparencies with grid lines on them (ask your teacher for them), or two clear plastic bags with grid lines drawn on them

---

» Vega, Denise, Uechi Ng and Kimberly King. *Plants*. Milwaukee: Gareth Stevens, 2002.
» NASA: Kids Science News Network: Why Do Plants Grow Upwards? http://ksnn.larc.nasa.gov/webtext.cfm?unit=plants
» Adventures of the Agronauts: Plants and Gravity: http://www.ncsu.edu/project/agronauts/mission2_8.htm

Steps to Success:

1. Soak the seeds in water overnight in the plastic cup.
2. Fill both sandwich bags with cotton balls.
3. Press the cotton balls down a bit. They will hold the sunflower seeds in place. The seeds will be spaced about 2 inches (5 centimeters) from each other.

Continued ➔

Step 6

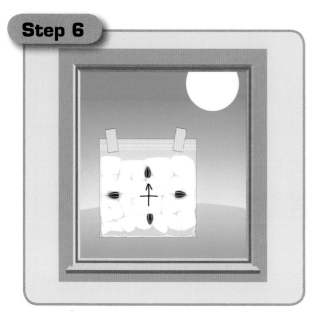

Step 9

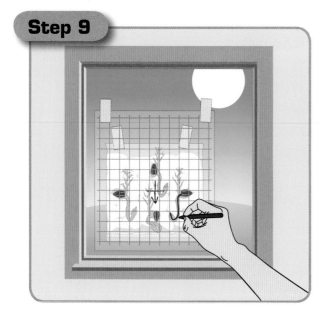

4. To position the first four seeds, think of the bag as a compass. The pointed side of the first seed should face "north." The pointed end of the second seed should face "south," toward the bottom of the bag. The pointed side of the third seed should face "east," and the pointed side of the fourth seed should face "west."

5. Dampen the cotton balls so they are moist. Seal the sandwich bag, and then use the pushpin to poke several airholes in it.

6. Draw an arrow pointing up on the bag to show the original direction of the bag. Tape the bag to a sunny window.

7. Repeat steps 4–6 with the remaining sunflower seeds.

8. Observe and record the position of the root and the stem of each seed over several days. Check the moisture level in the cotton balls and add more water if they seem dry. Be careful not to disturb the position of the seeds.

9. Once the roots and stems are a few centimeters long, turn one of the bags upside down and retape it to the window. Tape the gridded overhead transparencies to both bags. Mark any changes in the direction of growth over several more days.

Result Summary:

» Did all four seeds in each bag grow in the same direction?

» Did the direction of growth change as the roots and stems continued to grow?

» What effect did turning the bag upside down have on the roots and stems?

Added Activities to Give Your Project Extra Punch:

» Increase the number of bags of seeds used in this experiment. A larger sample will increase the accuracy of the results.

» Try using different kinds of seeds and compare their growth with that of the sunflower seeds.

» Turn grown plants upside down and compare the results with those you got with turning seeds upside down.

Display Extras:

» Decorate your board by gluing real seeds to it. Spray the seeds with shellac or another clear resin to preserve them.

» Include in your results the transparency grids you used to track the growth of each seed.

» Attach plastic or silk sunflowers to your board to create a border.

» Add sunflower seed packets to your board for a creative touch.

Cool Seeds

Plants have **adapted** to grow in many environments around the world—from the hot savannas in Africa to the cold steppes in Asia. Plants need light to **germinate,** or begin to grow. But do they also need heat? Do seeds in cold areas grow at a slower rate than those in warmer temperatures? Try this experiment to find out.

Do Your Research

In this experiment, you will be growing grass seed. Before you get started, do some research on plants, grasses, and the effect temperature has on them. You'll also need to know about **fluorescent lights,** which emit light without heating up. Once you've done some research, you might try this project or one of your own. You will need to use a refrigerator for this project, so check with your parents before you start. You'll also need an adult to supervise setting up the lights.

Here are some books and websites you could start with in your research:

» DK Publishing. *Plant.* New York: DK Children, 2004.

» Temperature Effect on Plants: http://www.ces.ncsu.edu/depts/hort/consumer/weather/tempeffect-plants.html

» How Fluorescent Lamps Work: http://home.howstuffworks.com/fluorescent-lamp.htm

Project Information

Possible Question:

Does temperature affect the rate at which plants grow?

Possible Hypothesis:

Plants will grow more slowly at lower temperatures.

Level of Difficulty:

Advanced

Approximate Cost of Materials:

$25

Materials Needed:

» Compass or other sharp tool
» Ten 3-ounce paper or plastic cups
» Potting soil, enough to fill ten 3-ounce plastic cups

Materials Needed (cont.):

» Grass seed, enough to evenly cover the soil in ten small plastic cups (about 75–100 seeds per cup)
» Two plastic storage containers, each big enough to hold five 3-ounce plastic cups
» Two 18-inch (46-centimeter) fluorescent lightbulbs and holders, or fluorescent lightbulbs and fixtures from an old aquarium
» Two shoeboxes
» Refrigerator
» Two thermometers
» Two flat extension cords
» Large light-proof box, or a closet kept at room temperature
» Ruler
» Adult supervisor

Steps to Success:

1. Use the compass to carefully poke a few holes in the bottom of each cup.

2. Fill each cup with potting soil to within ¾ inch (2 centimeters) of the top of the cup.

3. Spread the grass seeds in a single even layer over the potting soil in each cup.

4. Place five cups in each of the two plastic storage containers.

Continued →

5. Pour half a cup of water into each cup. Leave the water that drains through the bottom in the storage container.

6. Place each storage container in a shoebox, and then place a fluorescent light on the top of each box. Have an adult help you set up the fluorescent lights. Be sure to wash your hands after touching the soil.

Step 6

7. Put one box and light setup in the refrigerator, along with one thermometer. Wait about five minutes for the thermometer to cool, and then record the temperature. Arrange the extension cord for the light so the refrigerator door closes. If it won't close, try moving the cord along the refrigerator door until you find a place that lets the door close.

8. Put the other thermometer, box, and light setup in the light-proof box or in a room-temperature closet where sunlight cannot hit it. Record the temperature.

9. Observe the seeds twice daily. Add half a cup of water to each cup of seeds every three days. Record the day the grass germinates in each place. Once the grass begins to grow, use the ruler to measure the growth of five blades of grass in each cup. Then, record the average height of the grass in each cup.

10. Record the growth and temperature in each cup for several days. Compare the growth of the grass in both places.

Result Summary:

» Did the temperature remain constant in both places?
» Did the temperature affect the growth?
» Once the seeds germinated, did they grow at different rates because of the different temperatures?
» What other factors might have been involved?

Added Activities to Give Your Project Extra Punch:

» Show the average height of the grass in the five cups in each place on your results table.
» Research the type of grass seed you used to find out in which climate it grows best.
» Try using two different types of grass seeds in this experiment.
» Extend the amount of time the grass grows in each place.
» Decrease the amount of time the plants are under the light. Then, note the difference in results from the original experiment.

Display Extras:

» Show the growth rate in both table and graph forms.
» Check to see whether you can rig a fluorescent light to light up your board when you display it.
» Decorate your board with real grass seeds glued on to form a border.
» Cover the back of your board with a woven grass mat.

Too Much of a Good Thing?

Plants need **nutrients** to grow. Wild plants get nutrients on their own, but people add fertilizers to the plants grown in their homes and on farms. A recommended amount of fertilizer to be added to the plant is usually listed somewhere on the container. But, if a little fertilizer is good, wouldn't a little more be better? Try this experiment to find out.

Do Your Research

You'll need at least a month and a lot of sunlight to complete this project. Be sure to give yourself enough time. You will be adding different amounts of fertilizer to radish plants. It is best to use a liquid fertilizer because it will be easy to vary the amount of fertilizer used while keeping it evenly distributed. Ask your parents about the best place to store the fertilizer to keep it away from pets and young children. Before you begin this project, do some research about plants and the nutrients they need to grow. Learn about fertilizers, too. Once you've done some research, you can begin the project described here or create your own unique project.

Here are some books and websites you could start with in your research:

» DK Publishing. *Plant.* New York: DK Children, 2004.

» Kids World: A Homeowner's Guide to Fertilizer
http://www.agr.state.nc.us/cyber/kidswrld/plant/label.htm

» Kids World: Plant Nutrition
http://www.agr.state.nc.us/cyber/kidswrld/plant/nutrient.htm

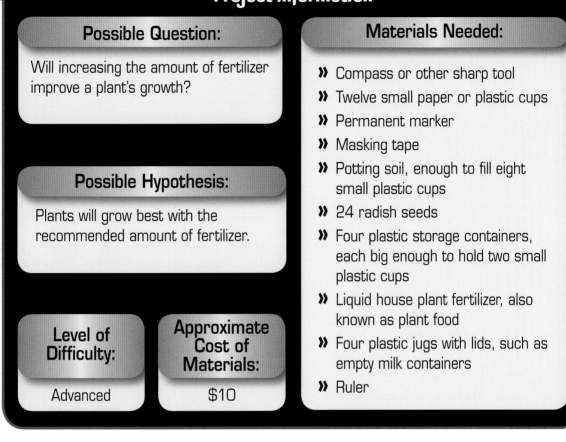

Project Information

Possible Question:

Will increasing the amount of fertilizer improve a plant's growth?

Possible Hypothesis:

Plants will grow best with the recommended amount of fertilizer.

Level of Difficulty:

Advanced

Approximate Cost of Materials:

$10

Materials Needed:

» Compass or other sharp tool
» Twelve small paper or plastic cups
» Permanent marker
» Masking tape
» Potting soil, enough to fill eight small plastic cups
» 24 radish seeds
» Four plastic storage containers, each big enough to hold two small plastic cups
» Liquid house plant fertilizer, also known as plant food
» Four plastic jugs with lids, such as empty milk containers
» Ruler

Steps to Success:

1. Use the compass to carefully poke a few holes in the bottom of eight of the plastic cups. Number the eight cups 1a and 1b, 2a and 2b, 3a and 3b, 4a and 4b. Add the following labels to the pairs of cups:
   a. 1a and 1b: water only
   b. 2a and 2b: recommended amount
   c. 3a and 3b: recommended amount x 1.5
   d. 4a and 4b: recommended amount x 2.0

2. Fill each cup with potting soil to within ¾ inch (2 centimeters) of the top of the cup. Place three radish seeds, evenly spaced, on the top of the soil in each cup. Gently cover each seed with a little soil.

3. Place one pair of the cups in each of the four plastic storage containers. Put all the containers in a sunny place.

Continued ⟶

4. Label the remaining cups 1, 2, 3, and 4. You will use them to water the plants.

5. Label the four jugs the same way you labeled the cups.

6. Prepare a different fertilizer-and-water mixture in each of the plastic jugs. The first jug has water only; the second is made with the recommended amount of fertilizer; the third is made with 50 percent more than the recommended amount; and the fourth is made with double the recommended amount.

7. Pour half a cup of water from jug 1 into cup 1. Use this to water the seeds in the cups labeled 1a and 1b. Leave the water that drains through the bottom in the storage container.

8. Repeat step 7 using the mixtures in the other three jugs and the cups with matching labels.

9. Check the seeds daily. Water them with the corresponding fertilizer mixture according to the instructions given on the fertilizer container. Usually, this is once per week. If the soil is dry to the touch, add half a cup of regular water.

10. Record the first day on which at least one radish seed germinates in each cup. Once the radish plants begin to grow, use the ruler to measure the growth of three plants in each container, and average your results.

Step 10

Plant Growth

	Day 1	Day 2	Day 3	Day 4	Day 5
Water Only					
Cup 1a					
Seed 1			germinate	0.8 cm	1.6 cm
Seed 2				germinate	0.8 cm
Seed 3				germinate	1.0 cm
Cup 1b					
Seed 1				germinate	0.8 cm
Seed 2				germinate	0.7 cm
Seed 3					germinate
Recommended Amount					
Cup 2a					
Seed 1			germinate	1.1 cm	2.0 cm
Seed 2			germinate	1.1 cm	2.2 cm
Seed 2			germinate	1.4 cm	2.4 cm

11. Continue to add fertilizer and record the plant growth in each cup for several weeks. Compare the growth of the radishes from each set of cups.

Result Summary:

» Which set of plants grew the tallest?

» Which set grew the least?

» Did any of the plants have unusual or unexpected growth patterns?

» Is there a connection between the amount of fertilizer used and the amount of growth recorded?

Added Activities to Give Your Project Extra Punch:

» Show the average height of the six radishes you grew in each container.

» Extend the amount of time you grow the radish plants to include growing a full radish. Measure the size of the radish grown with each fertilizer mixture.

» Use a different brand of fertilizer and note any differences in plant growth from what you observed in the original experiment.

» Research the ingredients of the fertilizer you used and describe their role in helping plants grow.

Display Extras:

» Decorate your board with packets of radish seeds and labels from the fertilizer you used.

» Show the growth of the radishes in both table and graph forms.

So Long, Starch

Leaves are a plant's manufacturing site. They are where sunlight, water, and carbon dioxide are used to make food for the plant in the form of starches and sugars. This process is called **photosynthesis.** Will a leaf continue to produce starch once sunlight is taken away? This project will show you.

Do Your Research

In this experiment you'll be using tincture of iodine, which you might find in your medicine cabinet to be used as a disinfectant. Be sure to keep it away from young children and pets. You will also need to boil leaves in water. Wear eye protection and make sure an adult is present when you are working with any heating element.

You'll need several large geranium leaves and a full day of sunlight. You'll be cutting the leaves off the plant, so be sure you have permission to do so. Before you begin, do some research on photosynthesis to find out more about starch production. You should also learn about iodine and its reaction to starch. Then, you'll be ready to try this project. Or, your research may lead you to try something else.

Here are some books and websites you could start with in your research:

» Farndon, John. *World of Plants – Leaves.* San Diego: Blackbirch, 2006.

» Hopkins, William G. *Photosynthesis and Respiration.* New York: Chelsea House, 2006.

» Photosynthesis: http://www.mcwdn.org/Plants/Photosynthsis.html

Project Information

Possible Question:

What will happen to starch production if a leaf is removed from sunlight?

Possible Hypothesis:

Starch production will stop after a few hours without sunlight.

Level of Difficulty:	Approximate Cost of Materials:
Advanced	$10

Materials Needed:

» Twelve geranium leaves
» Ten pieces of aluminum foil, each about 2 inches x 4 inches (5 centimeters x 10 centimeters)

Materials Needed (cont.):

» Ten paper clips
» Scissors
» Six plastic trays or plates
» Permanent marker
» Masking tape
» Safety glasses
» Hot plate
» Isopropyl alcohol (rubbing alcohol)
» Double boiler, or another pot and heat-proof container
» Water
» Oven mitts or pot holders
» Metal tongs
» Tincture of iodine
» Eyedropper
» Paper towels
» Adult supervisor

Steps to Success:

1. Choose ten leaves on the geranium plant that are well exposed to sunlight. Fold a piece of aluminum foil over each leaf so it is completely covered. Use the paper clips to hold the foil in place.

2. Immediately after clipping the foil in place, cut two leaves that have not been covered by aluminum foil.

Continued

3. Label the six plastic trays to correspond with the time you will be checking the leaves for starch:

    a. Test 1: Control
    b. Test 2: 2 hours
    c. Test 3: 4 hours
    d. Test 4: 6 hours
    e. Test 5: 8 hours
    f. Test 6: 24 hours

Step 4

4. Put on your safety glasses. With adult supervision, warm 100 milliliters of alcohol using a double boiler. Use oven mitts or pot holders to carefully set aside the pot of warmed alcohol. **Caution: Alcohol is flammable. Do not heat directly over an open flame.**

ADULT SUPERVISION REQUIRED

5. Return the pot of water to a boil.

6. Place the two cut leaves in the boiling water for five minutes. Boiling breaks down the leaf's cell walls.

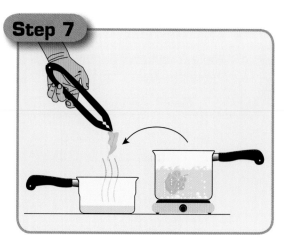

Step 7

7. Use the metal tongs to move the leaves from the boiling water into the alcohol for two minutes. The alcohol removes the chlorophyll from the leaf. This is done so you can clearly see the iodine-starch reaction.

8. Place the leaves on a paper towel and pat them dry. Then, transfer the leaves to the tray labeled Test 1: Control.

9. Use the eyedropper to put two or three drops of iodine on each leaf. Observe the leaves for one minute. The iodine should change color from orange to blue-black or purple as it reacts to starch in the leaves.

10. After two hours, boil water and heat the alcohol as directed in steps 4 and 5. Then, cut off two of the foil-covered leaves and repeat steps 6–9. Record your results.

11. Continue the procedure in step 9 for Tests 3–6 at the times listed. Compare the iodine color from each test.

12. Tightly cap the iodine and ask an adult to put it away. The used alcohol can go down the sink. Wrap the leaves in a paper towel before throwing them in the trash.

Result Summary:

» Did all the leaves cause the iodine to turn purple?
» Did the iodine not react on any of the leaves?
» Were there differences in the color changes?

Added Activities to Give Your Project Extra Punch:

» Research plant sources of starch in human diets.
» Try using leaves from different plants and compare their reaction time with that of the geranium leaves.
» Try the same experiment again at a different time of year. Compare the results with those from the original experiment.

Display Extras:

» Include photographs of the leaves after the iodine reacted to starch.
» Make a border using aluminum foil, paper clips, and leaves.
» Make a diagram showing the process of photosynthesis to include in your display.

Just Add Water

Seeds need the right conditions to begin growing. One important factor is water—without it, seeds cannot grow. How much water can seeds absorb? Is the amount of water related to a seed's size? You can find out by trying this experiment.

Do Your Research

Water is the first trigger for **germination,** the process in which seeds begin to grow. Before you begin this project, do some research on germination and seeds. Once you've done some research, you'll be ready to dig into this project. Or, you may come up with your own unique project after you've read and learned more about the topic.

Here are some books and websites you could start with in your research:

» Farndon, John. *World of Plants – Seeds.* San Diego: Blackbirch, 2006.

» Hopkins, William G. *Plant Development.* New York: Chelsea House, 2006.

» Great Plant Escape: Germination
http://www.urbanext.uiuc.edu/gpe/case3/c3facts3.html

» Biology of Plants: Starting to Grow: http://mbgnet.net/bioplants/grow.html

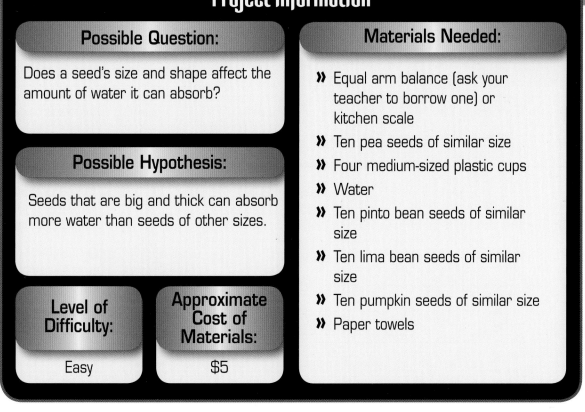

Project Information

Possible Question:

Does a seed's size and shape affect the amount of water it can absorb?

Possible Hypothesis:

Seeds that are big and thick can absorb more water than seeds of other sizes.

Level of Difficulty:

Easy

Approximate Cost of Materials:

$5

Materials Needed:

» Equal arm balance (ask your teacher to borrow one) or kitchen scale
» Ten pea seeds of similar size
» Four medium-sized plastic cups
» Water
» Ten pinto bean seeds of similar size
» Ten lima bean seeds of similar size
» Ten pumpkin seeds of similar size
» Paper towels

Steps to Success:

1. Place ten pea seeds on the scale.

2. Weigh the pea seeds. Find the average weight of one pea seed by dividing by ten. Record your results.

3. Put the pea seeds in a plastic cup and fill the cup with enough water to completely cover all the seeds.

4. Repeat steps 1, 2, and 3 with the pinto bean, lima bean, and pumpkin seeds. Let all the seeds soak for 24 hours.

Continued ⊕

Step 5

5. Before weighing the soaked pinto bean seeds, you'll need to get rid of any excess water that wasn't absorbed by the seeds. Gently remove the seeds from the cup and pat them dry with a paper towel. Then, weigh the soaked seeds. Find the average weight of one pinto bean seed by dividing by ten. Record your results.

6. Repeat step 5 for the other three types of seeds.

7. Find the percentage weight gain using this formula: Subtract the original weight from the new weight. Divide the difference by the original weight. Convert the result to a percentage by moving the decimal point two places to the right.

8. Compare the percentage weight gain of all four types of seeds.

Step 7

10 pumpkin seeds dry weight:
4 grams/10 seeds = 0.4g/seed

10 pumpkin seeds soaked weight:
9 grams/10 seeds = 0.9g/seed

$0.9 - 0.4 = 0.5$
$0.5 / 0.4 = 1.25$
$1.25 = 125\%$

Result Summary:

» Did all four seed types absorb the same amount of water?

» If not, which seed absorbed the most water? Which absorbed the least?

» Rank the seeds according to the percentage of water absorbed. Did one seed absorb a greater percentage of water than the others? Did the percentage of water absorbed have to do with the original weight of the seed?

Added Activities to Give Your Project Extra Punch:

» Research seed banks and how seeds are stored in them. Seeds can remain **viable** for years if they are kept in a dry environment.

» Try using different kinds of seeds in this experiment.

» Compare the amount of water each type of seed absorbed after one hour. Did the seed that absorbed the most water after one hour absorb the most water overall?

Display Extras:

» Show your results in both table and graph forms.

» Decorate your board with real seeds glued on to form a border. Spray them with shellac or another clear resin to preserve them.

» Attach empty packets of the seeds used in the experiment to add a creative touch.

Color My World

Light is essential for plant growth. Sunlight is the primary light source for plants on Earth. You may know that sunlight is really made up of different colors. But is any single color the best for plant growth? Let's find out.

Do Your Research

This project will take at least a month to complete, so be sure to give yourself enough time. Sunlight is made from a rainbow of light colors. Plants use sunlight to make food in a process called photosynthesis. Before you begin this project, do some research on photosynthesis and sunlight. Once you've done some research, you can tackle this project. Or, you may come up with your own unique project after you've learned more.

Here are some books and websites you could start with in your research:

» Juettner, Bonnie. *The KidHaven Science Library – Photosynthesis*. San Diego: KidHaven Press, 2005.

» Photosynthesis and Transpiration (Made Easy): http://www.cornwallwildlifetrust.org.uk/educate/kids/photsyn.htm

» Photosynthesis: http://library.thinkquest.org/3715/photo3.html

» Science, Optics and You: Newton's Prism Experiment: http://micro.magnet.fsu.edu/primer/java/scienceopticsu/newton/

Project Information

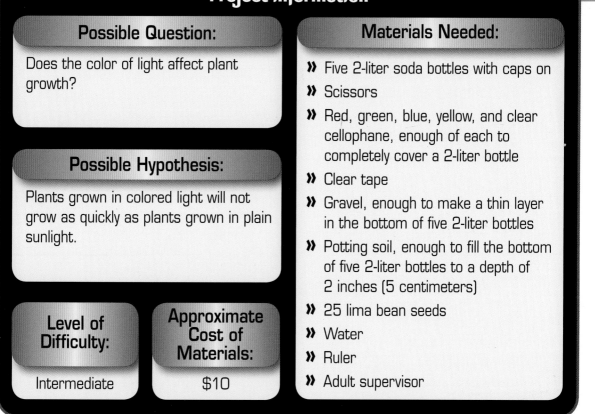

Possible Question:

Does the color of light affect plant growth?

Possible Hypothesis:

Plants grown in colored light will not grow as quickly as plants grown in plain sunlight.

Level of Difficulty:

Intermediate

Approximate Cost of Materials:

$10

Materials Needed:

» Five 2-liter soda bottles with caps on
» Scissors
» Red, green, blue, yellow, and clear cellophane, enough of each to completely cover a 2-liter bottle
» Clear tape
» Gravel, enough to make a thin layer in the bottom of five 2-liter bottles
» Potting soil, enough to fill the bottom of five 2-liter bottles to a depth of 2 inches (5 centimeters)
» 25 lima bean seeds
» Water
» Ruler
» Adult supervisor

Steps to Success:

Step 1

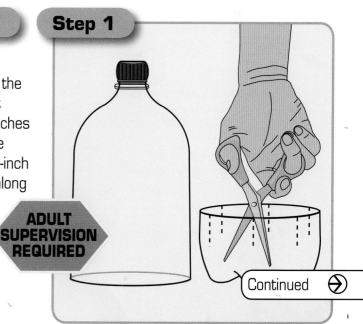

1. Remove the labels from the 2-liter bottles. Cut apart each bottle about 3½ inches (9 centimeters) from the bottom. Then, cut six ½-inch (1.25-centimeter) slits along the rim of the bottom so the top portion of the bottle can fit over it. Have an adult help cut the bottles. Trim any jagged edges.

ADULT SUPERVISION REQUIRED

Continued →

2. Cover the top of each bottle with a different color of cellophane. Use clear cellophane for growing the control group of seeds. Attach the cellophane to the bottle top with clear tape.

3. Spread a thin layer of gravel in the base of each bottle for drainage and to give the base extra weight. Then, add a layer of potting soil about 2 inches (5 centimeters) deep.

4. Gently push five lima bean seeds into the soil along the sides of each base so you can still see them through the plastic.

5. Add water to the soil so it is damp. Be sure to add the same amount of water to all five bases.

6. Cover each base with one of the tops that are now covered with cellophane, to make **terrariums.** Put all five terrariums in a sunny place. Do not add water; the terrariums should stay moist. Avoid exposing the plants to nonfiltered sunlight during the experiment.

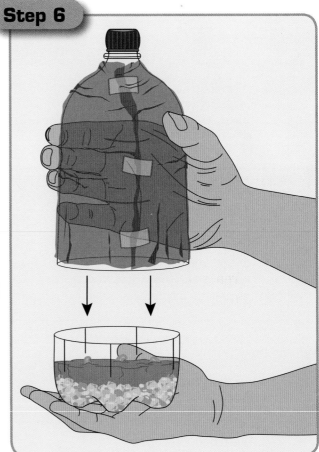
Step 6

7. Observe and record the growth of the seeds in each terrarium over several weeks. Compare the growth in the terrariums.

Result Summary:

» Did all the lima bean seeds in each terrarium germinate at the same time?

» Was there a difference in the growth rates from one terrarium to the next?

» Did all the lima beans in each terrarium grow at the same rate?

Added Activities to Give Your Project Extra Punch:

» Increase the number of seeds in each terrarium. More information increases the accuracy of the results.

» Try using other colors of cellophane, such as purple and orange.

» Experiment with other kinds of seeds and compare their growth with that of the lima bean seeds.

Display Extras:

» Show your results in both table and graph forms. The colors of your graphs could match the colors of the cellophane.

» Decorate your board by gluing real lima bean seeds to it. Spray the seeds with shellac or another clear resin to preserve them.

» Create artwork that shows light breaking into a spectrum as it goes through a prism. Add the rainbow prism art to your board.

Stem Straws

Plant stems have many functions. In addition to holding up the flower and storing food for the plant, they also transport water and nutrients. If the water is in the ground, how does a stem seem to defy gravity to bring the water to the top of the plant? How quickly does this happen? Do different plants move water at different rates? You can find the answers to these questions with this project.

Do Your Research

Stems have specialized cells called **xylem** that transport water. Water movement is due to a process called **transpiration,** in which water is transported from the stem's xylem cells to the leaves, where the water **evaporates.** Before you begin this project, do some research on stems and how water moves through a plant. Then, you can tackle this project or come up with your own unique project after you've read and learned more about the topic.

Here are some books and websites you could start with in your research:

» Bodach, Vijaya Khisty. *Stems.* Mankato, Minn.: Pebble Plus, 2006.
» Farndon, John. *World of Plants – Stems.* San Diego: Blackbirch, 2006.

Project Information

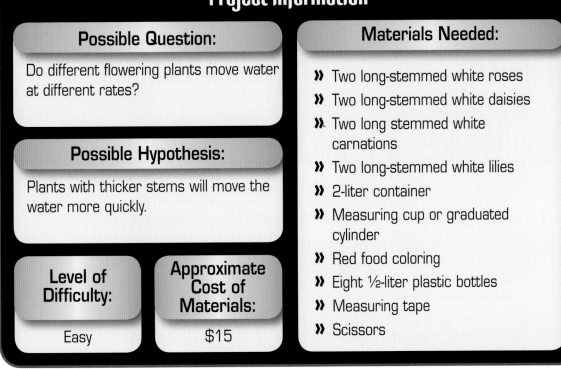

Possible Question:

Do different flowering plants move water at different rates?

Possible Hypothesis:

Plants with thicker stems will move the water more quickly.

Level of Difficulty:

Easy

Approximate Cost of Materials:

$15

Materials Needed:

» Two long-stemmed white roses
» Two long-stemmed white daisies
» Two long stemmed white carnations
» Two long-stemmed white lilies
» 2-liter container
» Measuring cup or graduated cylinder
» Red food coloring
» Eight ½-liter plastic bottles
» Measuring tape
» Scissors

» Stems: http://www.mcwdn.org/Plants/Stems.html
» Plant Nutrition: http://lgfl.skoool.co.uk/examcentre.aspx?id=256

Steps to Success:

1. While you are preparing your materials, keep your flowers in a container of water. Do your measuring and cutting as quickly as possible to avoid letting air into the stem bases.

2. Mix 2 liters of water with 100 drops of red food coloring (approximately one small bottle of food coloring).

3. Pour 50 milliliters of the red water into each of the eight ½-liter plastic bottles.

Continued ⊕

4. Use the measuring tape to find the flower with the shortest stem. Cut each stem at an angle about 1 inch (2.5 centimeters) above this length, so the length of each flower's stem is equal to that of the others. Quickly place each flower into one of the ½-liter bottles.

5. Keep the bits of stem you cut off. Measure each stem's diameter by standing the stem on end and tracing it on a sheet of blank paper.

6. Record the time at the beginning of the experiment.

7. Observe and record the color of the flowers every fifteen minutes. You will know the water has moved from the base of the stem into the flower when the flower begins to be tinged with red.

8. Continue your observations until all the flowers show a reddish color.

Step 7

Flower type:
Carnation #1
Diameter: 4mm

Date: 9/20
Start Time: 4:00 pm
15 min:
30 min:
45 min:
End time:

Amount of water absorbed

Result Summary:

» Did all four types of flowers become red at the same time?

» If not, what was the order of color change?

» Did the diameter of the stems have any bearing on the rate the water moved up them?

» What other factors might be involved? For example, did any stem have leaves on it? Were all the stems green or were some woody?

Added Activities to Give Your Project Extra Punch:

» After the first flower becomes red, remove one of each type of flower from its container. Then, measure the amount of water that remains in each container. The flower whose container has the least amount of water remaining moved the most water.

» Identify other factors that may have affected your results, such as the size of the flower or the number of leaves on the stem.

» Use a fan to create a breeze near the flowers. Observe whether moving air changes the results of your experiment.

Display Extras:

» Include "before" and "after" photographs of your flowers as part of your display.

» Show your results in both table and graph forms.

» Attach plastic or silk flowers of the kind used in your experiment to make a border.

» Attach the dried, red-tinged flowers you used in the experiment.

Undercover Color

Many leaves change color in the fall, going from dark green to brilliant reds, yellows, and oranges. Just where do these colors come from, and where does the green color go? Find out about leaf colors with this project.

Do Your Research

To prepare the leaves, you'll be crushing them in acetone (the chemical name for nail polish remover) and leaving them in the solution overnight. As with any chemical, keep acetone away from small children and pets. Wear safety glasses to protect your eyes during this procedure.

The green color of leaves is due to **chlorophyll,** a chemical necessary for photosynthesis to occur. The other colors are natural pigments in the leaf that are most prominent as the plant is ready to lie dormant for the winter months. It is best to do this project in late summer or early fall, just before leaves begin to change color. You will then need to wait until the leaves do change so you can compare the colors in your experiment with the colors of the fall leaves. Be sure to time your project to include the color change.

Before you get started, do some research on fall leaves and **chromatography,** the process you'll use in this experiment to determine the fall leaf colors. Once you've done some research, you can try this project or come up with your own unique project.

Project Information

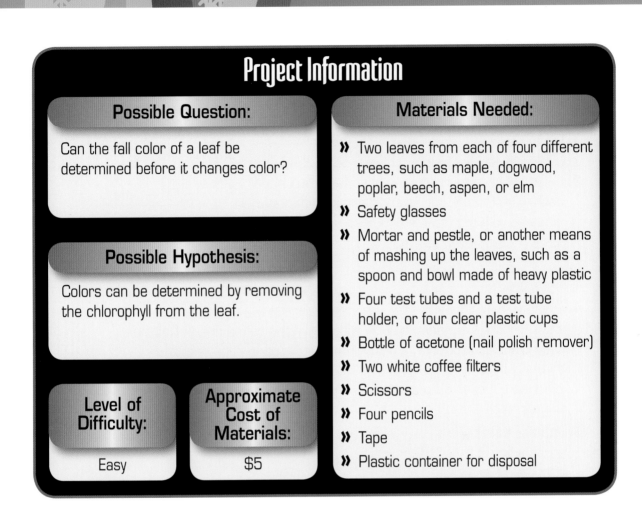

Possible Question:

Can the fall color of a leaf be determined before it changes color?

Possible Hypothesis:

Colors can be determined by removing the chlorophyll from the leaf.

Level of Difficulty:

Easy

Approximate Cost of Materials:

$5

Materials Needed:

» Two leaves from each of four different trees, such as maple, dogwood, poplar, beech, aspen, or elm
» Safety glasses
» Mortar and pestle, or another means of mashing up the leaves, such as a spoon and bowl made of heavy plastic
» Four test tubes and a test tube holder, or four clear plastic cups
» Bottle of acetone (nail polish remover)
» Two white coffee filters
» Scissors
» Four pencils
» Tape
» Plastic container for disposal

Here are some books and websites you could start with in your research:

» Bodach, Vijaya Khisty. *Leaves*. Mankato, Minn.: Pebble Plus, 2006.
» Farndon, John. *World of Plants – Leaves*. San Diego: Blackbirch, 2006.
» Why Leaves Change Color in the Fall:
  http://www.na.fs.fed.us/spfo/pubs/misc/leaves/leaves.htm
» Chromatography:
  http://acs.chem.ku.edu/Carnival2001/Activities/chromatography.asp

Continued →

1. Get permission to select a few leaves from trees before you begin collecting them. Note the location of the trees you are using for this project so you can check on the color of their leaves in fall.

2. Collect at least four varieties of leaves. You'll need two leaves of each type. Put on your safety glasses, and then mash up each pair of leaves with the mortar and pestle. Place one pair of mashed-up leaves in each test tube.

3. Cover the leaf mash with acetone. Allow the mixture to sit for 24 hours.

4. Prepare the coffee filters for the chromatography. Cut four strips, each ½ inch (1.25 centimeters) wide, from the coffee filters. Cut the base of the strip to form a point. Place one strip in each test tube so the pointed tip is just touching the acetone/leaf mixture. Tape the other end of each strip to a pencil and lay the pencil across the top of the test tube.

5. Observe the filter strips every 30 minutes for two hours and record your results. Make a final observation after 24 hours and note any changes. The strip in each test tube should have a green line, followed by one or more lines of different colors.

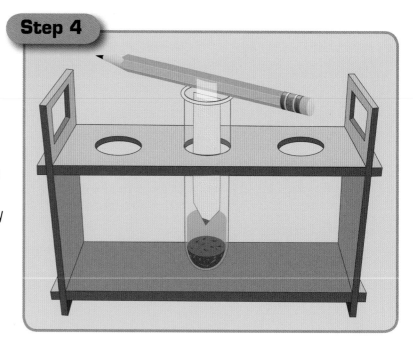

Step 4

6. When you are finished with your observations, put the acetone/leaf mixture into a plastic container, such as a milk jug, and dispose of it as hazardous waste. Contact your local sanitation district to find out how to do this in your area.

7. Compare these colors to the color of leaves from the same tree in the fall.

Result Summary:

» Did the filter strips remain white?
» If not, what colors did you see on the strips?
» Did the leaf colors match the fall colors of leaves from the same tree?

Added Activities to Give Your Project Extra Punch:

» Research the way in which chlorophyll is changed in leaves during the fall.
» Make a chart showing the average dates for fall color changes in your area.
» Try chromatography on leaves from several other trees or leaves from nonwoody plants.

Display Extras:

» Include the paper chromatography strips on your display board.
» Display both summer and fall leaves of each type of tree you used in your experiment.
» Include photos of the trees in the summer and in the fall, after their leaves change color.
» Make a chart showing the annual life cycle of a tree as part of your display.

Microwave Manipulation

Microwaves are part of our everyday life. We use microwaves to heat our food, send and receive messages, even guide airplanes. Microwave **radiation** is detected everywhere in the universe. So how does all this radiation affect plant growth? What will happen to seeds when they are exposed to microwaves from a microwave oven?

Do Your Research

This project requires at least four weeks to finish. Make sure you have planned enough time to complete it. You'll also need an adult to approve the use of the microwave and to supervise when you are heating seeds. Before you begin this project, do some research to find out more about plants and different kinds of microwave radiation. Then, you can try this project or you may come up with your own version.

Here are some books and websites you could start with in your research:

» Hopkins, William G. *Plant Development*. New York: Chelsea House, 2006.
» Morgan, Sally. *Green Plants*. Chicago: Heinemann, 2006.
» NASA: Microwave Effects on Plant Growth:
  http://www.nasa.gov/centers/ames/news/releases/2003/03_94AR.html
» What Are Microwaves?
  http://www.ieee-virtual-museum.org/exhibit/exhibit.php?id=159265&lid=1

Project Information

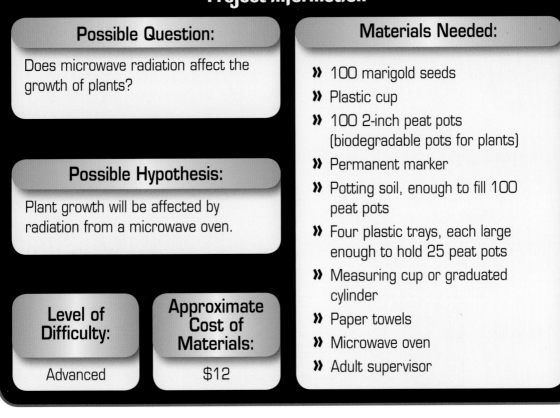

Possible Question:

Does microwave radiation affect the growth of plants?

Possible Hypothesis:

Plant growth will be affected by radiation from a microwave oven.

Level of Difficulty:

Advanced

Approximate Cost of Materials:

$12

Materials Needed:

» 100 marigold seeds
» Plastic cup
» 100 2-inch peat pots (biodegradable pots for plants)
» Permanent marker
» Potting soil, enough to fill 100 peat pots
» Four plastic trays, each large enough to hold 25 peat pots
» Measuring cup or graduated cylinder
» Paper towels
» Microwave oven
» Adult supervisor

Steps to Success:

1. Soak all the seeds in water overnight in the plastic cup.
2. While you are soaking the seeds, label the peat pots as follows:
   a. Label 25 pots M-10 for "microwaved 10 seconds."
   b. Label 25 pots M-20 for "microwaved 20 seconds."
   c. Label 25 pots M-30 for "microwaved 30 seconds."
   d. Label 25 pots M-0 for "microwaved 0 seconds." This will be your control group.
3. Fill all the peat pots with potting soil. Plant the 25 control seeds in the M-0 pots according to the directions on the seed packet. Place the pots on one of the four plastic trays; water each pot with about 50 milliliters of water. Leave the water that drains through in the tray.

(Continued ➔)

4. You are now ready to microwave the rest of the seeds. With an adult supervising, place 25 seeds on a paper towel in the microwave. Microwave the seeds at full power for 10 seconds, and then plant them in the M-10 peat pots. Place the pots on a tray; water as you did for the control group.

ADULT
SUPERVISION
REQUIRED

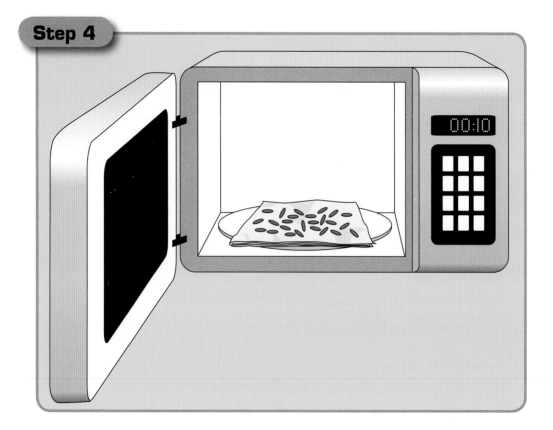

Step 4

5. Repeat step 4 with 25 new seeds, but microwave them for 20 seconds and plant them in the pots labeled M-20.

6. Repeat step 4 with the remaining 25 seeds, but microwave them for 30 seconds and plant them in the pots labeled M-30.

7. Place all the trays in a sunny place. Water the pots with the same amount of water when the soil is dry to the touch.

8. Record the date that each seed germinates. After two weeks, record the total number of seeds that germinated from each group.

Result Summary:

» Did all the seeds germinate?
» If not, which group of seeds had the greatest number of germinated seeds?
» Which group germinated in the least amount of time?
» Which group took longest to germinate?

Added Activities to Give Your Project Extra Punch:

» Continue the experiment to determine whether microwave radiation affects the growth of the marigold plants.
» Try using different kinds of seeds and compare the effect of radiation with the effect on the marigold seeds.
» Double the amount of time each seed is microwaved. Use caution: The seeds might get very hot. Compare the results with those of your original experiment.
» Test what would happen if the seeds were exposed to other forms of radiation. For example, you could ask your dentist to let you put some seeds on top of your lead apron the next time you get your teeth X-rayed!

Display Extras:

» Show your results in both graph and table forms.
» Make a "microwave door" out of cardboard and attach one side of it to your board. Glue some marigold seeds on a paper towel behind the door, so when you open the door, the seeds are inside.
» Add marigold seed packets to your board for a creative touch.

The Competition

Learning is its own reward, but winning the science fair is pretty fun, too. Here are some things to keep in mind if you want to do well in the competition:

1) Creativity counts. Do not simply copy an experiment from this or any other book. You need to change the experiment so that it is uniquely your own.

2) You will need to be able to explain your project to the judges. Being able to talk intelligently about your work will help reassure the judges that you learned something and that you did the work yourself. You may have to repeat the same information to different judges, so make sure you've practiced it ahead of time. You will also need to be able to answer the judges' questions about your methods and results.

3) You will need to present your materials in an appealing manner. Discuss with your teacher whether or not it is acceptable to have someone help you with artistic flourishes to your display.

Keep these guidelines in mind for your display:

» **Type and print:** Display the project title, the question, the hypothesis, and the collected **data** in clean, neatly crafted paper printouts that you can mount on a sturdy poster display.

» **Visibility:** Be sure to print your title and headings in large type and in energetic colors. If your project is about the Sun, you might use bright reds, oranges, and yellows to bring your letters to life. If your project is about plant life, you might use greens and browns to capture an earthy mood. You want your project to be easily visible in a crowd of other projects.

» **Standing display:** Be sure your display can stand on its own. Office supply stores have thick single-, double-, and triple-section display boards available in several sizes and colors that will work nicely as the canvas for your science fair masterpiece. Mount your core data—your discoveries—on this display, along with photos and other relevant materials (charts, resource articles, interviews, etc.).

» **Attire:** Dress neatly and comfortably for the fair. You may be standing on your feet for a long time.

4) The final report is an important part of your project.
   Make sure the following things are in your final report:

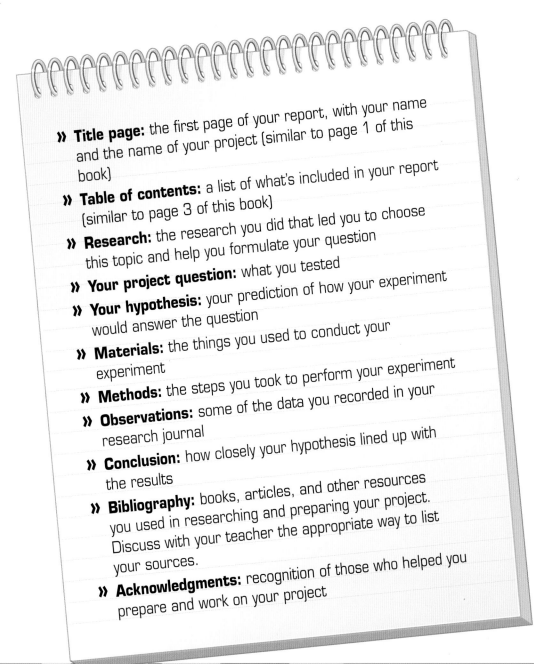

» **Title page:** the first page of your report, with your name
and the name of your project (similar to page 1 of this
book)

» **Table of contents:** a list of what's included in your report
(similar to page 3 of this book)

» **Research:** the research you did that led you to choose
this topic and help you formulate your question

» **Your project question:** what you tested

» **Your hypothesis:** your prediction of how your experiment
would answer the question

» **Materials:** the things you used to conduct your
experiment

» **Methods:** the steps you took to perform your experiment

» **Observations:** some of the data you recorded in your
research journal

» **Conclusion:** how closely your hypothesis lined up with
the results

» **Bibliography:** books, articles, and other resources
you used in researching and preparing your project.
Discuss with your teacher the appropriate way to list
your sources.

» **Acknowledgments:** recognition of those who helped you
prepare and work on your project

Prepare to be Judged

Each science fair is different, but you will probably be assigned points based on your performance in each of the categories below. Make sure to talk to your teacher about how your specific science fair will be judged. Ask yourself the questions in each category to see whether you've done the best possible job.

Your objectives
» Did you present original, creative ideas?
» Did you state the problem or question clearly?
» Did you define the variables and use controls?
» Did you relate your research to the problem or question?

Your skills
» Do you understand your results?
» Did you do your own work? It's OK for an adult to help you for safety reasons, but not to do the work for you. If you cannot explain the experiment, the equipment, and the steps you took, the judges may not believe that you did your own work.

Data collection and interpretation
» Did you keep a research journal?
» Was your experiment planned correctly to collect the data you needed?
» Did you correctly interpret your results?
» Could someone else repeat the experiment by reading your report?
» Are your conclusions based only on the results of your experiment?

Presentation
» Is your display attractive and complete?
» Do you have a complete report?
» Did you use reliable sources and document them correctly?
» Can you answer questions about your work?

Glossary

adapted changed in order to be suitable to live under specific conditions

chlorophyll green coloring in plants that is necessary for photosynthesis

chromatography technique for separating materials

control sample in an experiment that is left unchanged and used for comparison with other samples that have variables

data factual information

evaporates changes from a liquid into a vapor or gas

fluorescent light glass tube in which light is produced by gases that react to an electric current

geotropism growth in response to gravity

germinate begin to grow; sprout

germination the first stage in development of a seed into a plant

hypothesis scientific idea about how something works, before the idea has been tested

nutrients chemicals that plants and animals need for growth and development

photosynthesis process in green plants in which carbon dioxide, water, and sunlight are used to create nutrients for the plant

prediction say in advance what you think will happen, based on scientific study

radiation energy output in the form of waves or rays

scientific theory belief based on tested evidence and facts

terrarium closed container used for growing plants

transpiration process in which plants lose water

tropism reaction of a plant due to external stimuli, such as light or gravity

variable something that can change; is not set or fixed

viable able to live

xylem tissue found in some plants for transporting water

Index